Ripley's SPORTS

Believe It or Not!®

PUBLISHING

a Jim Pattison Company

TWISTS

Written by Geoff Tibballs
Consultant Stewart Newport

PUBLISHING

Publisher Anne Marshall

Editorial Director Rebecca Miles
Project Editor Lisa Regan
Editor Rosie Alexander
Assistant Editor Charlotte Howell
Picture Researchers James Proud, Charlotte Howell
Proofreader Judy Barratt
Indexer Hilary Bird

Art Director Sam South
Senior Designer Michelle Cannatella
Design Rocket Design (East Anglia) Ltd
Reprographics Juice Creative Ltd

www.ripleys.com/books

Copyright ©2010 by Ripley Entertainment Inc.

First published in Great Britain in 2010 by Random House Books,
Random House, 20 Vauxhall Bridge Road, London SW1V 2SA
www.rbooks.co.uk

Addresses for companies within The Random House Group Limited
can be found at: www.randomhouse.co.uk/offices.htm

The Random House Group Limited Reg. No. 954009

CONTENTS

TWISTS

PAGE 13

WORLD OF SPORT

So you think you know about sport? Well, prepare to learn even more! Top sports attract millions of spectators and billions of pounds, and bring together countries across the globe to play, watch and shout about their favourite games and competitions.

Sport isn't just about big money, clubs and players. Some sports are played and watched by only a few people, but are just as much fun. So, if you're not into ball games, this book will introduce you to tug-of-war, BMX racing, and even worm charming. There's something here for everyone…

WHAT'S INSIDE YOUR BOOK?

Do the twist

Take a look…each page is packed with sporting superstars, amazing achievements, and of course, crazy pastimes that don't get a mention in other sports books. That's what a Twists book is all about!

TWISTS

Don't forget to look out for the 'twist it!' column on some pages. Twist the book to read snappy sports stories from all around the world; if you're feeling super sporty then read it standing on your head!

twist it!

Welsh footie fan Steve Thatcher named his son after all the players in his favourite team, Cardiff City. It means young Sam has 12 middle names!

A rough game, and players are allowed to elbow, kick, and even head butt each other!

27 players dressed in 16th-century costume. It is a rough game, and players are allowed to elbow, kick, and even head butt each other!

An annual football match called the Calcio takes place in Florence, Italy, between two teams of 27 players dressed in 16th-century costume.

An annual football match called the Calcio takes place in Florence, Italy, between two teams of 27 players dressed in 16th-century costume.

by nearly 200,000 spectators.

final between Brazil and Uruguay was watched by nearly 200,000 spectators.

Important football matches often attract crowds of over 70,000 people, but the 1950 World Cup final between Brazil and Uruguay was watched by nearly 200,000 spectators.

an incredible 48 kicks and lasted nearly an hour!

Cup tie in Africa, the penalty contest went on for an incredible 48 kicks and lasted nearly an hour!

Some football matches are decided by penalty shoot-outs, where eight kicks are often enough to get a result. At the end of a 2005 Namibian Cup tie in Africa, the penalty contest went on for an incredible 48 kicks and lasted nearly an hour!

SPEEDY SPORTS

Sport isn't all about speed – but speed certainly makes sport exciting! See what's fastest in the world of sport…

Motorbike 580 km/h

Formula 1 Car 414 km/h

Learn fab fast facts to go with the cool pictures.

Ripley explains some of the science and know-how behind your favourite sports.

Say what? Oh, so that's what that word means...

SURF'S UP

RIDING THE WAVES

Ripley explains...

You catch a wave by pushing the water toward the back of the surfboard with your hands, moving you forward. As you ride on the wave the water rises beneath you and pushes you forward faster and faster. All the time gravity is trying to push you down, while buoyancy is pushing you up.

It's not only waves that are a danger to surfers. Each year as many as 50 surfers are attacked by sharks.

...surfers rode the same wave at the same time off the coast of Brazil in 2007.

Have you ever wished you could ride a wave on a surfboard? Some waves are huge—up to 70 feet high. That's more than four times the height of an adult giraffe! That just makes it even more a challenge... surfer. You can surf a ...standing or lying down—and some ...on the same wave for half an ... just do what you enjoy.

...8th century —used planks of ...weight polyurethane ...California, Florida, ...bed and strong...

RIDING HIGH

Kite surfers use wind power to help them speed across the water and soar up to 162 feet in the air. They stand on a board and hold on to a large controllable kite. The aim is to do tricks such as jumps, spins, and even somersaults, and to see how high and long they can jump off waves.

CATCH A WAVE

This is when you launch yourself into the path of a suitable wave.

SAY WHAT?

Kite surfers can go great distances when the wind is behind them. In 2006, UK kite surfer Kirsty Jones traveled 140 miles from Lanzarote in the Canary Islands to Morocco.

Windsurfers attach a sail to their surfboards. When the wind blows into the sail from behind, it makes the board go faster: sometimes up to 60 mph! Windsurfers can perform amazing stunts, jumps, and spins.

Donald "D.J." Dettloff has created a colorful fence from more than 700 surfboards near his home in Hawaii.

Ripley's Believe It or Not!

Lauren Miller's dog Auggie liked to do tricks with tennis balls. He could pick up five in his mouth at the same time!

Twists are all about 'Believe It or Not!' — amazing facts, feats, and things that will make you go 'Wow!'

Look for the Ripley 'R' to find out even more than you knew before!

Motorbike Wheelie	Ostrich	Camel	Racehorse	Human (sprinter)
225 km/h	72 km/h	64 km/h	64 km/h	37 km/h

SPEED KINGS

The cars reach speeds of nearly 400 km/h on the straights.

Imagine flying a plane at over 3,000 km/h. Or riding a motorbike at 600 km/h. Or driving a speedboat at 500 km/h. Wow! Ever since vehicles were invented, people have wanted them to go as fast as possible. We love speed. That's why we dream of one day racing in NASCAR or driving in a Formula-1 race. The cars there can go from 0 to 160 km/h and back to 0 in under five seconds.

Jamaica's Usain Bolt doesn't need an engine to go fast. He can run at amazing speeds. In 100-metre races he averages just under 40 km/h but for a few strides he actually reaches 50 km/h. That's the speed limit for a car in most towns!

Three drivers (AJ Foyt, Al Unser and Rick Mears) have won four Indy 500s.

The Indy 500 is probably the most famous motor race in the world. About 400,000 people turn up to watch, and millions more see it on TV in more than 160 countries. The 500-mile (805-kilometre) race takes place every year at the oval-shaped Indianapolis Motor Speedway in Indiana.

CRAZY CORNERING

As they go round corners, motorbike racers lean their machines at almost impossible angles of 50 degrees without falling off. The riders have their knee just a few centimetres off the ground to work out how much they can lean before their bike loses balance and topples over.

HIGH SPEED FURNACE

Fire-proof balaclava

Formula-1 drivers need to be amazingly fit. The temperature in the car reaches 50°C and drivers get very hot beneath their fire-proof overalls. They lose an average of 2 kg in body weight during each race. When braking and cornering, the pull on the driver's neck is so great that it feels as if their head wants to roll off their shoulders!

Flame-resistant driving suit

When the Indy 500 was first raced in 1911, the track was made up of 3.2 million bricks, earning it the nickname 'The Brickyard'.

MOTORHEADS

The first car race was run in France from Paris to Rouen in 1894. The average winning speed was just over 17 km/h!

English farmer George Shields drives a garden shed that can do 90 km/h. He once drove it all the way from one end of Britain to the other. That's nearly 1,300 km.

CG Mouch of Los Angeles fitted the front end of a 750cc Honda motorcycle to the rear end of his lawn mower to create a 'chopper mower' that could mow the lawn at up to 15 km/h.

The 1972 Bandama Car Rally in West Africa was so tough that none of the 52 starters finished the race.

In 2005, Australian Matt Mingay did a motorbike wheelie at a speed of 225 km/h.

TWIST IT!

LIGHTNING BOLT

Jamaican runner Usain Bolt won the 100 metres at the 2008 Beijing Olympics in an incredible 9.69 seconds — despite slowing down to celebrate and having his left shoelace undone!

ON FOUR LEGS

ANIMAL ATHLETES

Racehorses are bred for speed. These thoroughbreds, as they are known, can gallop at up to 65 km/h. Horse-racing dates back nearly 3,000 years to the ancient Greeks who added the spectacular sport of chariot racing to the Olympics in 680BC. Horse-racing is so popular today that in Switzerland there is even a horse race on ice, run on a frozen lake.

There are also races for animals that you might not think are built for speed, such as camels, armadillos, pigs and sheep. Whatever the animal, there is probably a race for it somewhere in the world. We don't only race animals. We wrestle them, we ski behind them, and in parts of Asia polo is played on elephants instead of horses.

HORSE POWER

In the Palio, which takes place twice each summer, horses race at breakneck speed three times around the main square in Siena, Italy – and the riders don't even have saddles to sit on. No wonder so many fall off!

Around 60,000 people squeeze into the square to watch the colourful race.

The Palio was first raced in 1656 and has remained largely the same ever since.

A bank of mattresses is positioned to protect the horses and riders from the walls of a café at a turn known as the 'corner of death'.

Jockeys are usually small, but they also have to be strong, because racehorses can weigh up to 700 kg.

DERBY

A derby is a type of race. The original derby was a horse race run in Epsom, England, and was named after the Earl of Derby who founded the event in 1780.

JUMBO POLO

Polo is usually played on horseback but in countries such as Nepal, India and Thailand they play it with elephants. Two people ride each elephant – one to steer the elephant, the other to hit the ball. The mallet used to strike the ball is made of bamboo and can be up to 3.7 m long, depending on the height of the elephant. If a player falls off, it's a long way down!

RACING AROUND

The Frog Derby takes place in Rayne, Louisiana, where kids dress frogs in miniature jockey uniforms! By tapping the ground behind the frogs, they encourage them to hop along the course in leaps and bounds.

At an annual round-up in Stephensville, Wisconsin, participants try to wrestle slippery, squirming pigs to the ground in thick mud.

You may have heard of greyhound racing. Well, in Oklahoma City, they have a dog race with a difference – it's for little dachshunds and it's called the Dachshund Dash.

Back in 1937, a man in England tried to stage cheetah racing as an alternative to greyhounds. The cheetahs showed no interest in running, however, and often just stood still.

twist it!

A racehorse named Camarero won 56 races in a row in Puerto Rico between 1953 and 1955.

<< PIG OLYMPICS >>

It's not only humans that have their own Olympics. There is also an Olympic Games for pigs! Miniature pigs run over hurdles, compete in swimming races and play a version of football called pigball, where they chase a ball covered in fish oil with their snouts.

DESERT DERBY

In the Middle East and Australia, camel racing is a serious sport with big prize money. Top racing camels sell for up to £30,000. Camels can run as fast as 65 km/h in short sprints and can maintain a speed of 30 km/h for an hour. Jockeys need nerves of steel because the camels can sometimes suddenly stop mid-way through a race without warning!

MAKING A SPLASH

WET AND WILD

Water isn't a person's natural element: our lungs need air, we don't have webbed feet or hands, and we aren't designed for speed in the way that a shark or a seal is. That hasn't stopped us from taking the plunge, though.

Free divers plummet to depths of more than 180 m using only their finely tuned athlete's bodies. Marathon swimmers race over distances of up to 25 km in lakes, rivers or the ocean. Competition divers perform graceful gymnastics before hitting the water at around 55 km/h. They're all spectacular.

Taking a dive

Competitive divers perform twists or somersaults in mid-air after jumping from a platform up to 10 m above the pool. They have just a split second to get everything right. They must enter the water with their body in a vertical position and their arms extended forward – and without making much of a splash.

PROFESSOR SPLASH

From heights of up to 25 m, Darren Taylor, of Denver, Colorado, dives into tiny, shallow pools, some containing just 30 cm of water! He says the secret is to make a real splash when he lands – that way his fall is cushioned. The impact still leaves his body so bruised that it hurts him to laugh for weeks afterwards.

SAY WHAT?

FREESTYLE

In a freestyle race swimmers can use any style – front crawl, butterfly, backstroke or breaststroke. Most use the front crawl, because it's the fastest.

DIVE IN!

Once a diver has left the board, his or her body must be held in one of four positions.

STRAIGHT: no bend in either the hips or knees

PIKE: knees straight and the body bent at the waist

TUCK: the body is curled up in a tight ball

FREE: a combination of straight, pike or tuck with the legs together

HIGH DIVE

Tom Daley became the world 10-metre platform diving champion in 2009 at the age of just 15. That made him the youngest diver ever to win a title in men's platform diving. He started diving at age seven and was Britain's youngest competitor at the 2008 Olympic Games.

Absolutely nuts

Twiggy the grey squirrel is nuts about water-skiing. Her Florida trainer, Lou Ann Best, taught her to be towed around an inflatable paddling pool by a remote-controlled model boat at speeds of up to 10 km/h. Twiggy has demonstrated her skills at boat shows across America.

It's never too late to start a sport. As a child, Australia's Ian Thorpe was allergic to chlorine (the chemical used in swimming pools), so he didn't swim in his first race until he was seven. Even then the allergy forced him to swim awkwardly with his head out of water.

SLOW STARTER

His nickname was 'the Thorpedo' because of his speed in the water.

By age 14 Ian Thorpe was representing his country.

TRIALS OF STRENGTH

FEEL THE FORCE

Some people are so strong they can bend iron bars with their head or pull trains with their teeth. Others can lift cars off the ground, tear thick books with their bare hands or pull trucks with their hair. For centuries, people have demonstrated their strength by taking part in competitive combat sports such as boxing, sumo wrestling, judo, taekwondo and karate.

If you don't want to be a real-life muscle man, you could take part in some wackier trials of strength. How about having a go at fish tossing, welly hurling or mobile-phone throwing?

It took Rev. Fast 1 minute 16 seconds to pull the plane 8.8 m with a rope.

The Globemaster weighed a huge 187 tonnes.

The previous record for pulling a plane was 186 tonnes and had stood for 12 years.

He trains for his strong-man challenges by pulling his pickup truck up hills.

Strong stomach

Fitness instructor Ken Richmond has such a sturdy stomach he lets people fire cannon balls at it! He can also survive a cannon ball being dropped on his head and withstand the force of a massive 18,000-kg wrecking ball slamming through a concrete wall and into his amazing abdomen.

PLANE CRAZY

In 2009, Reverend Kevin Fast, of Cobourg, Ontario, Canada, managed to pull an enormous military CC-17 Globemaster airplane across the tarmac at Canadian Forces Base Trenton.

FAST MOVER

Wrist

Knifehand

Contact Points used in Karate

Back of the hand

Spearhand

Ball of the foot

Instep

In the Japanese martial art of karate, you can punch or kick but the most famous technique is the knifehand or karate chop. Some people can smash over 30 slabs of concrete with just a single karate chop.

Ripley's Believe It or Not!®

🌀 American martial arts movie star Bruce Lee moved his arms and feet with lightning speed. He was so fast he could snatch a coin off a person's open palm before they could close it, and leave a different coin behind.

🌀 To toughen the skin on his fists, he used to regularly thrust his hands into buckets of rocks and gravel up to 500 times.

🌀 He could break wooden boards that were 15 cm thick with a single punch.

🌀 He could perform one-handed push-ups using only his thumb and index finger.

🌀 He could thrust his fingers through unopened fizzy drink cans.

🌀 He practised his high kicks by jumping up and tapping people on the ear with his foot.

EARS!

Zafar Gill, from Pakistan, can lift 55 kg with one of his ears.

EYES!

Dong Changsheng, from China, once pulled a 1,700-kg minibus carrying two adult passengers... with his eyelids!

TOUGH TEETH

Luxembourg's Georges Christen can do just about anything with his teeth. He has towed a 95-tonne ship with them, and bent 368 nails with them in an hour. One stunt saw him stop three 110-horsepower Cessna Sport airplanes from taking off at full power – one with his teeth and two with his arms.

twist it!

In New Zealand, there is an annual contest to see who can throw a gumboot (wellington boot) the farthest. At the end of the competition, the winner is presented with a Golden Gumboot!

In Michigan in 1997, Samoan heavyweight boxer Jimmy Thunder knocked out Crawford Grimsley after just 1.7 seconds of their fight.

The first Mobile Phone Throwing World Championships were held in Finland in 2000. One of the sport's top throwers is the UK's Chris Hughff who can hurl a phone 95.7 m. That's a real long distance call!

STRONG STUFF

Ed Byrne from England used his bare hands to karate chop through 55 concrete blocks in less than five seconds...and it didn't even hurt!

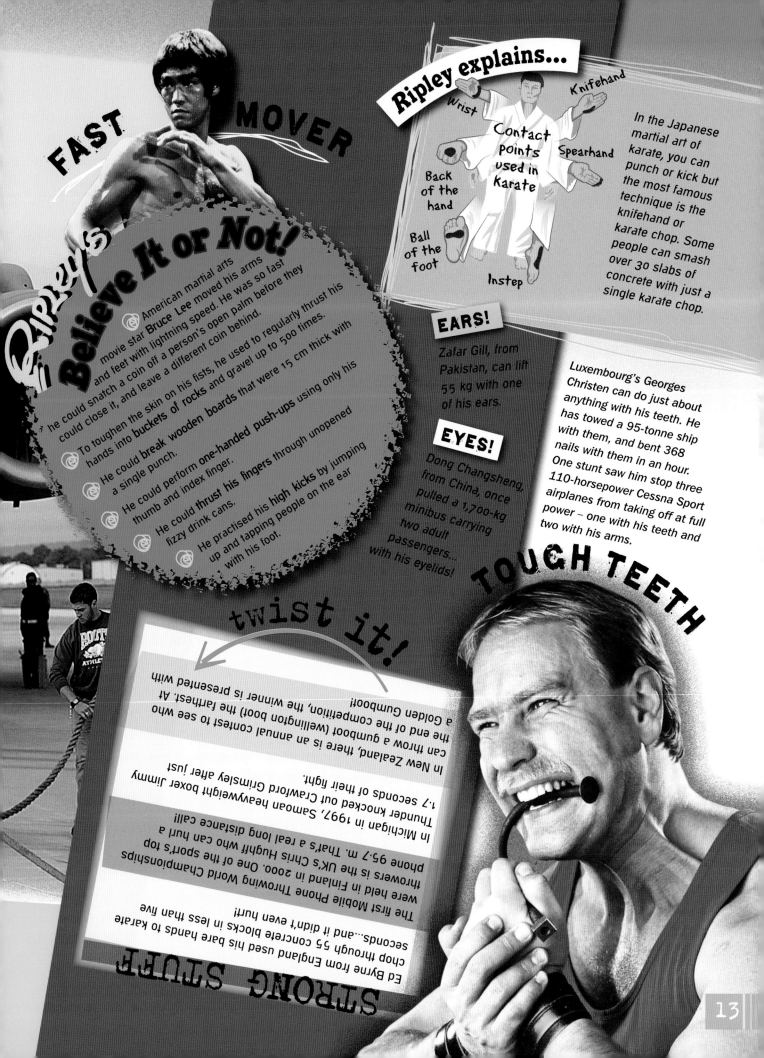

ON COURT

Michael was so feared that opponents would put two or even three men to cover him every time he touched the ball.

More than 46 million Americans play volleyball and there are around 800 million players worldwide. In fact, football is the only sport that more people play across the globe. Like basketball, tennis, squash and badminton, volleyball is played on a court. All of these sports require you to be able to run about, have quick reactions, and be very fit. Tennis players can cover 8 km during a match!

Tennis players can also earn a lot of money. The winners of the singles titles at Wimbledon in London (the world's oldest tennis tournament) receive £1 million. Basketball players can earn even more. Some get paid over £13 million a year!

GROWTH SPURT

At high school, Michael Jordan was considered too short to play basketball. Then he grew 10 cm one summer, and began the path to superstardom that saw a 1996 sports magazine name him the greatest athlete of the past 50 years. He finished with an incredible career total of 32,292 points, the third highest in league history.

High court

Top tennis players Roger Federer and Andre Agassi needed a head for heights when they played on this court. It was marked out on the helipad of a Dubai hotel 210 m above ground. If a ball sailed out, nobody went to fetch it!

PLAYING BALL

America's Andy Roddick can serve a tennis ball at 250 km/h – that's as fast as an express train.

A game of volleyball that took place in Amstelveen, the Netherlands, in 2008 lasted 60 hours. That's 2½ days!

Basketball-crazy Mike Campbell made 1,338 free throws in an hour (faster than one throw every three seconds) and over 90 per cent of his shots were successful.

Twin brothers Ettore and Angelo Rossetti played a continuous tennis rally that lasted nearly 15 hours, with a total of 25,944 shots.

Joseph Odhiambo dribbled a basketball through the streets of Houston, Texas, for 26 hours in 2006.

You have to be really fit to play squash. A squash player can burn up to 1,000 calories during a one-hour game. That's almost twice as many than if you were doing push-ups non-stop for the same amount of time. Phew!

IN A SPIN

Using his hands, feet, knees, and even his mouth, American Bruce Crevier can spin up to 21 basketballs at the same time. He has also spun a single basketball on his fingers for more than 22 hours – that's nearly a whole day!

twist it!

SMASHING!

Badminton is played by hitting a shuttlecock made either from goose feathers or plastic. Shuttlecocks can be hit very hard and very fast. A smash by China's Fu Haifeng was recorded at 370 km/h.

SISTER ACT

Venus Williams and her younger sister Serena have dominated women's tennis in the 21st century. Between them they have won over 30 Grand Slam titles.

Venus was docked a point when a string of beads scattered around the court. Venus's dreadlocked hair and Australian Open tennis tournament fell from her At the 2007 US Open, Venus served at 208 km/h – the second-fastest women's serve ever recorded.

SNOW AND ICE

CHILLS AND THRILLS

If you've ever sped down a hill on a sledge, you'll know how exciting snow can be. Wherever there is suitable snow and ice, sportspeople can be found competing on it. Speed skiers can hit a breathtaking 240 km/h, ski jumpers leap 180 m while sailing through the air at 105 km/h, and teams on bobsleighs hurtle around a steep course of solid ice at 145 km/h. They all know that the slightest mistake could result in a bad injury.

It's not all about speed. There's the gracefulness of ice skating, the elegance of snowboarding, and the rough and tumble of hockey. So if you thought the best thing about snow was building a snowman, you might have to think again.

SNOW TRICKS

Snowboarding is like surfing on snow. Boarders perform lots of tricks. In a U-shaped trench called a halfpipe, they do acrobatic spins and flips and even a trick where they grab their board in mid-air.

DOWNHILL RACERS

Slalom skiers speed down a steep mountain, weaving their way between a series of poles called gates. Nets are placed alongside the course at the most dangerous places but the skiers still have spectacular falls.

LOONY LUGE

Luge is one of the most dangerous sports. Competitors lie down on a fibreglass sledge and hurtle feet-first down an icy track at speeds up to 145 km/h. They wear little protection, their bodies are just centimetres from the ice, and the luge has no brakes!

ICE BOWLING

The coolest game of bowling takes place in Japan. Players roll a bowling ball made of ice along a frozen 5-m lane towards 17-cm-high ice pins.

Between 2003 and 2006, American Rainer Hertrich skied for 1,000 days in a row. He once hiked up an active volcano in Chile because it had more snow to ski down than neighbouring mountains!

WAYNE'S WORLD

Canadian Wayne Gretzky is the only National Hockey League player to total over 200 points (goals and assists) in a season, and he did it four times. He scored over 100 points in 14 consecutive seasons and was so popular that he used to receive 1,000 fan letters every month.

 At the Montreal Ice Cup, riders race bicycles over a course of sheet ice. They get a grip on the slippery surface by putting up to 400 screws into the rubber tyres.

OFF THE WALL

UNUSUAL SPORTS

The World Games is held every four years and features several unusual sports that aren't in the Olympics. These include canoe polo, dragon boat racing, climbing, tug of war, roller hockey, and even dancing. If you prefer your sports a little less energetic, have you ever thought about taking up worm charming or cherry pit spitting? There are many weird and wonderful sports that you can try wherever you live.

PULLING POWER

In tug of war, two teams of eight grip tightly on to either end of a 35-m-long rope and use their combined strength to pull their opponents over a line. Tug of war was practised as early as 500BC by Greek athletes and was an Olympic sport until 1920.

MIGHTY MUSCLES

A Japanese bodybuilder flexes her muscles at the 2009 World Games. Nearly 3,000 athletes from 84 countries took part in the Games.

PIE IN THE SKY

A Canadian and two Australians battle to catch the Frisbee during the flying disc competition at the World Games. The sport can be traced back to the Frisbie Pie Company in Connecticut, where workers played a game in which they threw empty pie tins to one another!

SPORTS CRAZY

At the World Flounder Tramping Championships in Scotland, people catch fish using their bare feet. They wade into the river and when they feel the flat fish wriggling between their toes, they pick it up. The person who catches the most fish is declared the winner.

If you've got something to shout about, you can do it at the National Hollerin' Contest, held each year at Spivey's Corner, North Carolina. Contestants yell as loud as they can for four minutes – you might want to take ear plugs!

At the Sheep Counting Championships of Australia, several hundred sheep are encouraged to run across a field while competitors try to count them.

twist it!

SPIT THE PIT

Like many established sports, cherry pit spitting started as a casual pastime and has developed into a popular event in which people compete at national and international competitions. At the 2006 World Championship in Germany, Franz-Wolfgang Coersten spit a pit an impressive 19.3 m.

THE EARLY BIRD

The World Worm Charming Championships have taken place since 1980 in Willaston, Cheshire, England. Competitors coax earthworms to the surface by wiggling garden forks in the soil or by pouring water on it. The winner is the person who brings the most worms to the surface in half an hour. In 2009, 10-year-old Sophie Smith won the first prize with a grand total of 567.

MOOoo

POOOO

COW PATTY BINGO

In some rural areas of North America you can play cow patty bingo. A field is divided into numbered squares, and contestants bet on which square the cow will take a poop!

POLE POSITION

To be crowned pole-sitting champion, you need a head for heights and a lot of patience. In 2002, Daniel Baraniuk won $20,000 (about £13,000) after spending 196 days and nights (over six months) on top of a 2.5-m-high pole. His closest rival fell off a month earlier!

TOUCH DOWN

CATCH AND KICK

Each year American football's biggest game, the Super Bowl, is watched on US TV by nearly 100 million people. American football grew out of the sport of rugby, which was invented in the UK in the early 19th century. Both American football and rugby use an oval-shaped ball. When the ball hits the ground, its odd shape means that it can bounce in any direction.

To play American football or rugby, you need to be strong or fast – better still if you are both. American football is played in other parts of the world, too, including Japan, Mexico and Europe.

Ripley explains...

NFL players have had to wear helmets to protect their head since the 1940s.

Shoulder pads are made of shock absorbing foam with a hard plastic cover. These protect the players and also make them look much bigger than they really are!

Plastic knee pads fit into pockets inside the football trousers. They protect the players' knees when they crash to the ground.

ROUGH AND TUMBLE

American football is fun and fast but also very physical with a lot of body contact. Around 40,000 high-school players suffer concussion (a mild head injury) every year playing football. Quarterbacks or running backs, who are tackled most often, rarely get through a season without being injured.

SCHOOLBOY ERROR

Rugby began in 1823 when William Webb Ellis, a student at Rugby School in England, caught the ball during a game of football and ran towards the other team's goal. It is now played in over 100 countries worldwide.

Oooooofff!

GRRRRR

72

<<THE FRIDGE>>

William Perry, a popular defensive lineman for the Chicago Bears, was known as 'The Fridge' because of his 1.88-m, 173-kg square body. Yet at high school he could leap high enough to dunk a basketball!

twist it!

his own one-yard line.
finally grabbed by one of his team-mates on his
ran 70 yards towards his own end zone. He was
picked up a fumble, lost his sense of direction, and
California Golden Bears in the 1929 Rose Bowl, he
for running the wrong way! When playing for the
American footballer Roy Riegels became famous

cushion to stop him from getting a sore behind.
in 2008. He sat for 12 hours each day and took a
the Pasadena Rose Bowl over a period of five days
Jim Purol of California sat in all 92,542 seats at

been left with no legs after a railway accident.
Michigan, despite being only 0.9 m tall. He had
Flint Southwestern Academy High School team,
Willie McQueen was a great defence tackler for

in a row from 1992 to 2004.
High School, Concord, California, won 151 games
The boys' American football team at De La Salle

he wore it every day for over four years.
Packers' jersey with Brett Favre's No 4 – that
was so excited by his 2003 Christmas gift – a
David Witthoft, a young Green Bay Packers' fan,

END ZONE

The French national rugby team have a live cockerel as their mascot. Sometimes he even attends the team's training sessions. It gives them something to crow about!

Rooster booster

21

PEDAL POWER

Wheels can have up to 48 spokes to help deal with bumpy landings.

Riders can pedal forwards and backwards for tricks.

The handlebars can spin in a circle.

BMX magic

BMX (Bicycle Motocross) began in southern California in the 1970s, but is so popular that in 2008 it became an Olympic sport. The bikes are designed for performing tricks and for racing on hilly dirt tracks. Riders must wear a full-face helmet, elbow pads, knee pads and shin guards. Yet even the best riders sometimes get hurt. American Mat Hoffman has had over 50 operations and 500 stitches, and broken almost every bone in his body.

There are so many different sports you can do on a bike. Racing cyclists zoom around a track at nearly 80 km/h. Cyclo-cross competitors ride through woods and across such rough land that they have to get off and carry their bikes up steep hills. BMX bikers are able to perform fantastic jumps and acrobatic twists in mid-air. In 2008, Kevin Robinson of the USA soared 8.2 m into the air on a BMX bike – equal to jumping over a three-storey building.

There are endurance races, too. At the Lotoja race in the USA, riders cover 330 km in a single day. Other people ride bikes down glaciers and mountains, and even ride them backwards – sometimes playing a musical instrument at the same time!

In the Netherlands there are more bicycles (16 million) than there are people.

twist it!

Austrian Marcus Stoeckl rode a mountain bike down a snow-covered mountain in Chile, reaching a speed of 210 km/h.

At the Down the Hill bike race in Taxco, Mexico, competitors ride mountain bikes through a house! They go in through a door, ride down a flight of stairs, and exit through another door.

Jumping from a ramp, Australian Nathan Rennie cleared over 36 m on his mountain bike in 2005.

At the 2009 X Games in Los Angeles, Anthony Napolitan performed two complete somersaults in mid-air to land the first-ever double front flip on a bicycle.

During the 1904 Tour de France – the world's most famous cycle race – French spectators sprinkled broken glass on the road so that the leaders would get punctures and allow their local favourite to win.

Balancing act

Ripley explains...

When you pedal a bike, you use your muscles to create a force. You are like the engine for your bike. Bicycles are so efficient they can convert 80 per cent of the energy you supply at the pedals into energy that powers you along. To compare, a car engine converts only 25 per cent of the energy in petrol into useful power.

It's scary enough riding a bike around volcano craters or on cliff tops, but Canada's Kris Holm does it on a unicycle! The one-wheeled daredevil has ridden on the rail of a 60-m-high bridge, the edge of a 805-m-high cliff, and within 10 m of red-hot, bubbling lava on a volcano in Hawaii.

COASTING ALONG

With an oxygen tank on his back, Maaruf Bitar of Lebanon practises his favourite hobby – underwater cycling – off the coast of the Mediterranean city of Sidon. Underwater cyclists have ridden at depths of over 60 m beneath the sea, that's 30 times the depth of an Olympic swimming pool.

EXTREME ACTION

Who would think you could play Scrabble underwater or iron a T-shirt at the top of a mountain? You can, thanks to a new range of extreme sports designed to make gentle pursuits or boring jobs much more exciting.

Instead of doing their ironing in the living room, some people do it in caves, in a canoe, on top of a statue, in the middle of a forest, or while snowboarding. It has become so popular that now you can even play Wii extreme ironing – back in your living room!

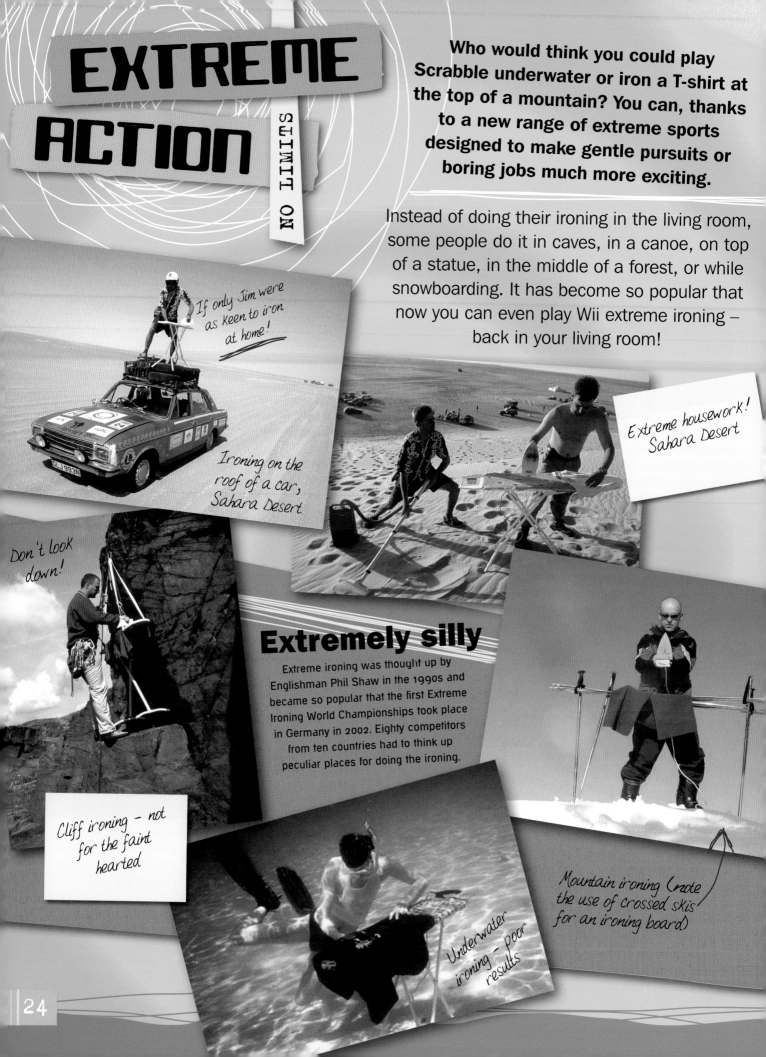

If only Jim were as keen to iron at home!

Ironing on the roof of a car, Sahara Desert

Extreme housework! Sahara Desert

Don't look down!

Extremely silly

Extreme ironing was thought up by Englishman Phil Shaw in the 1990s and became so popular that the first Extreme Ironing World Championships took place in Germany in 2002. Eighty competitors from ten countries had to think up peculiar places for doing the ironing.

Cliff ironing – not for the faint hearted

Underwater ironing – poor results

Mountain ironing (note the use of crossed skis for an ironing board)

EXTREME SCRABBLE

To celebrate the 60th anniversary of Scrabble in 2008, extreme enthusiasts played in some crazy places. Skydivers Nicole Angelides and Ramsey Kent played Scrabble at 4,000 m above Florida. With each move, they had to glue the tiles to the board to stop them blowing away.

BOUNCE

Fred Grzybowski of Los Angeles, California, can jump over a car on a pogo stick. The extreme pogo rider is able to bounce 2.4 m into the air and can also perform an incredible nine consecutive pogo backflips. The world championship called Pogopalooza attracts over 60 riders from the USA, Canada and the UK. The best riders can perform over 220 bounces in a minute.

twist it!

INSANE IRONING

- Two South Africans ironed while hanging from a rope across a 30-m-wide mountain gorge.

- A British pair did some ironing at a height of 5,425 m on Mount Everest.

- In 2007, Henry Cookson dragged his iron and ironing board 1,770 km across the frozen wastes of Antarctica.

- Australian Robert Fry threw himself off the side of a cliff in the Blue Mountains with an iron, a board, some laundry and a parachute!

- In 2009, 86 British scuba divers ironed underwater at the same time – in water as cold as -2°C.

ABOVE AND BEYOND

American Peter Jenkins has started a new sport – extreme tree climbing. He and his friends climb trees and perform acrobatic stunts. These include balancing on the branches and running across the canopy (the top) of the trees. They also tree surf, where they go high into the tree on a windy day and ride the branches like waves.

On a 2006 tour, extreme cello players Clare Wallace, Jeremy Dawson and James Rees carried their musical instruments on to the roofs of 31 different cathedrals in England and played a short concert on each.

In 2008, while orbiting in the International Space Station at 8 km a second, Canadian astronaut Greg Chamitoff played a game of extreme chess against a team of US students on Earth.

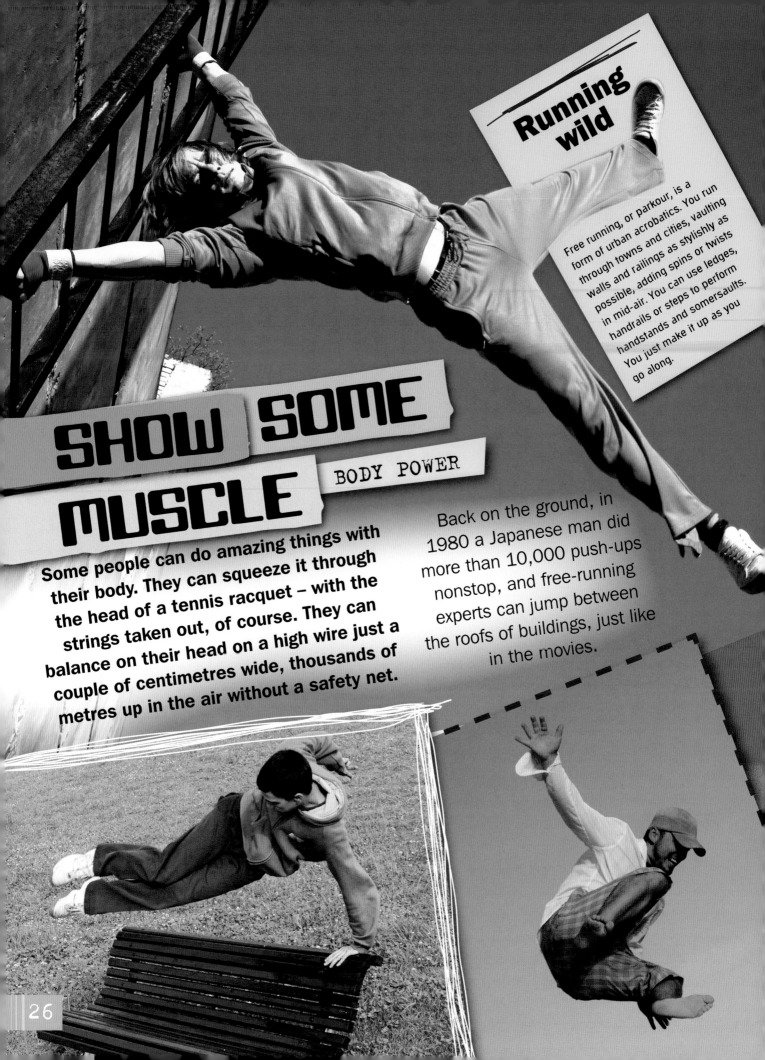

Free running, or parkour, is a form of urban acrobatics. You run through towns and cities, vaulting walls and railings as stylishly as possible, adding spins or twists in mid-air. You can use ledges, handrails or steps to perform handstands and somersaults. You just make it up as you go along.

SHOW SOME MUSCLE

BODY POWER

Some people can do amazing things with their body. They can squeeze it through the head of a tennis racquet – with the strings taken out, of course. They can balance on their head on a high wire just a couple of centimetres wide, thousands of metres up in the air without a safety net.

Back on the ground, in 1980 a Japanese man did more than 10,000 push-ups nonstop, and free-running experts can jump between the roofs of buildings, just like in the movies.

IN A SPIN

Kareena Oates from Australia is able to rotate 100 hula hoops around her body at the same time. She has also spun 41 hula hoops around her waist while suspended in the air by her wrists.

UP, UP, UP...

At the Tarragona Castells festival in Spain, acrobats climb over each other to form amazing human towers. There have been as many as ten levels of people standing on each other's shoulders, but sometimes the whole thing just comes crashing down.

Canadian gymnast and acrobat Dominic Lacasse held himself horizontally on a bar as a 'Human Flag' for 39 seconds, a display of incredible strength.

HUMAN FLAG

twist it!

ENERGY BUZZ

American Don Claps can perform more than 1,200 consecutive cartwheels, and he can even carry on doing them while drinking water from a paper cup!

In 2009, Davit Fahradyan of Armenia completed 354 arm-aching turns on a horizontal bar.

New Yorker Ashrita Furman hula hooped underwater for 2 minutes 20 seconds at a Florida dolphin centre in 2007. He used a special metal hoop and was able to breathe air through scuba-diving equipment.

Olga Berberich completed 251 jumps with a rope in just one minute in Germany in 2007.

Contortionist Daniel Browning-Smith, of Los Angeles, California, is so flexible he can squeeze his entire body into a box the size of a microwave oven.

Working in shifts of two people at a time, eight boys, aged between eight and 11, bounced nonstop on an inflatable castle in Michigan for 24 hours in 2008.

GET YOUR SKATES ON

American skater Rob Dyrdek once did 215 ollies in a row.

In 2006, Welshman Dave Cornthwaite spent 90 days on a skateboard, riding it all the way across Australia – a distance of more than 5,600 km! Skateboarders love to try new challenges. One man jumped over four cars on a skateboard, and another built a skateboard so big that nearly 30 people could stand on it at the same time.

There are now more than 18 million skateboarders in the world. You could also try roller hockey, speed skating, or if you can really stretch your arms and legs, the latest Indian craze of limbo skating!

Dude!

The ollie is one of the most popular aerial skating tricks. You bend down, push your back foot down on the tail end of the board and then allow the board to pop back up. As you leap into the air, the board appears to be stuck to your feet, as if by magic.

GREAT SKATES

Skateboarding was born when Californian surfers wanted something to surf on when the waves in the sea were flat. Believe it or not, top skaters have reached speeds of nearly 100 km/h.

DANNY'S WAY

In Mexico City in 2006, American skater Danny Way landed a sensational backflip, which he called El Camino ('The Way'). He sped down a 23-m-high ramp and leaped 21 m through the air at a speed of 80 km/h. The previous year he had jumped over the Great Wall of China on a skateboard. Not bad for someone who says he is afraid of heights!

Roller skates first became popular in the 1880s.

The lowdown

Limbo skaters have to be strong and flexible to skate under more than 50 parked cars at a time. They practise for months to get their body into the right position. Young limbo skater Aniket Chindak can roller-skate under cars that are just 24 cm off the ground.

TURNING HEADS

At the 1999 X Games, American Tony Hawk became the first skater to land a 900: that's 2½ rotations in mid-air.

Bingo, a Border collie, used to ride through the streets of Winnipeg, Canada, on a skateboard picking up litter.

In 2000, Richie Carrasco completed 142 dizzying 360-degree spins on a skateboard without stopping.

A roller skate invented by Frenchman M Mercier in the 1900s was powered by a two-cylinder petrol engine. This enabled the skater to zoom along at speeds of 30 km/h.

Around 280 roller skaters held on to the waist of the person in front of them to form a giant skating chain that snaked through the streets of Singapore City in 2006.

Rohan Ajit Kokane is so good at limbo skating he can do it under cars while blindfolded!

twist it!

SPEED SKATER

German inline skater Dirk Auer reached incredible speeds of nearly 300 km/h while being dragged behind a high-powered motorbike. Dirk is used to extreme skating and has also managed to skate along the roof of an airborne plane and down a rollercoaster.

Ripley's Believe It or Not!®

ROLLER MAN

Frenchman Jean-Yves Blondeau wears a special plastic suit with sets of rollers attached. It means he can roll down the motorway at nearly 100 km/h. He can even overtake motorbikes!

29

GOAL CRAZY

FANTASTIC FOOTBALL

About 3.5 billion people either play or watch football, making it the world's most popular sport. Every country plays the game, right down to tiny islands. On the Isles of Scilly, off the southwest coast of England, the league is made up of just two teams who play each other every week! It does mean the draw for the cup is not very exciting...

Football is fast and skilful. Some people love the game so much they name their children after their favourite players, dye their hair in their team's colours, or travel thousands of miles just to watch their team. The best players are treated like superstars and are paid over £100,000 a week. Boys and girls play football, but you need to be fit to be a professional, as some top players run up to 10 km during a match.

GOAL CRAZY

Freezing Footie

Jungfrau Mountain — Switzerland

International footballers staged a 2007 exhibition match on an artificial pitch laid out on a glacier. It took place in the shadow of Switzerland's 4,160-m Jungfrau Mountain. The high-altitude air was so tiring that the teams played just five minutes each half.

AL CRAZY

Dan Magness — Britain

Using his feet, thighs, chest and head, Britain's Dan Magness kept a football in the air for 24 hours. He touched the ball around 250,000 times, knowing that the smallest lapse in concentration would mean he would have to start all over again!

FREE KICKS

Some football matches are decided by penalty shoot-outs, where eight kicks are often enough to get a result. At the end of a 2005 Namibian Cup tie in Africa, the penalty contest went on for an incredible 48 kicks and lasted nearly an hour!

Important football matches often attract crowds of over 70,000 people, but the 1950 World Cup final between Brazil and Uruguay was watched by nearly 200,000 spectators.

An annual football match called the Calcio takes place in Florence, Italy, between two teams of 27 players dressed in 16th-century costume. It is a rough game, and players are allowed to elbow, kick, and even head butt each other!

Welsh footie fan Steve Thatcher named his son after all the players in his favourite team, Cardiff City. It means young Sam has 12 middle names!

twist it!

GOAL CRAZY

Nani

GOOOAAALLLlll

Portuyal

Portuguese football star Nani performs his famous backflip celebration after scoring a goal for Manchester United. The fans love it – as long as he doesn't injure himself doing it.

GOAL CRAZY

Tiny Field

Microscopic

Created by technology, this football pitch is so tiny that 20,000 of them could fit on the tip of a single human hair. It has all the markings of a full-sized pitch but can only be viewed using a really powerful microscope.

GOAL CRAZY

The Legendary Pelé

Pelé

Brazil

The great Brazilian footballer Pelé scored 1,281 goals in his career – more than any other professional player. He helped his country to win the World Cup three times, and scored the opening goal in the 1970 final when Brazil beat Italy 4–1.

GOAL CRAZY

Brainy Ball

Adidas

Germany

Adidas has designed a clever football. It contains a chip that sends a radio signal to the referee's watch in less than a second of the ball crossing the goal line. So there should be no more arguments about whether or not a shot was a goal.

GOAL CRAZY

On the Head

Manoj Mishra

India

Indian footie fan Manoj Mishra won a competition by balancing a ball on his head for 14 hours. He practised still yoga exercises so that he could get used to keeping still for so long. Afterwards he dedicated his success to his hero, Argentinian football legend Diego Maradona.

FLYING HIGH

TAKING TO THE SKIES

Many humans love to fly. As we don't have wings like a bird, we try the next best thing and take up sports such as hang gliding, paragliding, ballooning, gliding and skydiving. **American skydiver Don Kellner has made over 36,000 jumps, and Jay Stokes once made 640 jumps in a single day! Skydivers free fall at 200 km/h before the safety parachute opens and they descend gently to the ground.**

If you are worried about heights, you don't have to go up alone. You could always take your dog with you. Brutus, a miniature dachshund from California, made more than 70 jumps with his owner!

Mike Howard, an airline pilot, walked along a 5.8-m-long pole from one balloon to another, in 2004. When he had blindfolded and 1,200 m above Bristol, England, the daring tightrope walk, he completed the parachuted to the ground.

Although skydiving looks dangerous, in the USA there is only one death for every 100,000 jumps.

YEEE-HAAA…

WAA-HOOOO…

JUMP!

Skydivers jump from airplanes, helicopters and even hot-air balloons. Once their parachutes are open, they control their direction by pulling toggles on the end of steering lines attached to the chute. That's how they can land on a small cross marked on the ground after jumping from 4,000 m.

Buddy the Labrador and his owner, Bill Kimball of San Diego, California, went hang gliding together for more than eight years. Buddy joined Bill on over 75 flights.

twist it!

In Japan they stage kite fights. Competing teams tie sharp razor blades and broken glass to the tail strings of their kites and fly them against one another. The aim is to rip the opposing kite to shreds so that it can no longer fly.

In just eight days, Englishman Martin Downs skydived on six continents: Africa, Europe, South America, North America, Australia and Asia.

Vijaypat Singhania flew a hot-air balloon to an incredible altitude of 21,027 m over India in 2005.

In 2004, Bob Holloway flew 4,152 km in a powered paraglider from Astoria, Oregon, to Washington, Missouri.

Holly Budge from England skydived over Mount Everest in 2008. She jumped from a plane at 8,990 m and reached speeds of 225 km/h and braved temperatures of −40°C.

SUPERFLY GUYS

Ripley explains...

Rigging

Harness

Sail

Control Bar

Hang gliders can stay thousands of metres in the air for hours, soaring through the skies like an eagle. A hang glider has a lightweight aluminium frame, a big nylon wing, and no engine. The pilot is attached to the frame by a harness. There are no switches or buttons to worry about. Pilots steer by shifting their body weight on the frame, then all they have to do is relax and admire the views.

<<human bird>>

American Jeb Corliss comes as close as any human has to flying. Wearing a special winged jumpsuit, he takes part in the scary sport of proximity wingsuit flying. He jumps from a helicopter or off a cliff edge thousands of metres up and flies terrifyingly close to mountain faces. Jeb once flew down the 4,478-m-high Matterhorn Mountain in Switzerland, within just 1.5 m of the jagged cliff-face, and reached speeds of 160 km/h.

SURF'S UP

RIDING THE WAVES

It's not only waves that are a danger to surfers. Each year as many as 80 surfers are attacked by sharks.

84 surfers rode the same wave at the same time off the coast of Brazil in 2007.

Ripley explains...

Ripley explains...

You catch a wave by pushing the water towards the back of the surfboard with your hands, moving you forwards. As you ride on the wave the water rises beneath you and pushes you forwards faster and faster. All the time gravity is trying to push you down, while buoyancy is pushing you up.

Have you ever wished you could ride a wave on a surfboard? Some waves are huge – over 20 m high. That's more than four times the height of an adult giraffe! That just makes it even more of a challenge for a surfer. You can surf a wave standing up, crouching or lying down – and some surfers have managed to stay on the same wave for half an hour. There are no rules, you just do what you enjoy.

The first surfers – in Tahiti in the 18th century – used planks of wood, but today's surfboards are made of lightweight polyurethane foam. Surfing is really popular in places like California, Florida and Hawaii, where the shape of the seabed and strong winds create big waves.

RIDING HIGH

Kite surfers use wind power to help them speed across the water and soar up to 50 m in the air. They stand on a board and hold on to a large controllable kite. The aim is to do tricks such as jumps, spins and even somersaults, and to see how high and long they can jump off waves.

SAY WHAT?

CATCH A WAVE
This is when you launch yourself into the path of a suitable wave.

Kite surfers can go great distances when the wind is behind them. In 2006, UK kite surfer Kirsty Jones travelled 225 km from Lanzarote in the Canary Islands to Morocco.

Donald 'DJ' Dettloff has created a colourful fence from more than 700 surfboards near his home in Hawaii.

PLAIN SAILING

Windsurfers attach a sail to their surfboards. When the wind blows into the sail from behind, it makes the board go faster: sometimes up to 100 km/h! Windsurfers can perform amazing stunts, jumps and spins.

Ripley's Believe It or Not!®

In California they have a surfing contest that's just for dogs. Four-legged surfing dudes show their style on their own and with human partners. The winner receives a basket full of dog treats.

35

IN THE RUNNING

MARATHONS

People can't run as fast as cheetahs, but they can run much further. They need great stamina to do this. The longest running race in the Olympics is the marathon at just over 26 miles (42 km).

Just running a marathon is exhausting, but some athletes need greater challenges. So they run extreme (ultra) marathons that are a mega 160 km long. Occasionally, someone will even run all the way around the world – with lots of stops, of course!

The first marathon

In 490BC, Pheidippides, a Greek soldier, ran about 25 miles (40 km) from the town of Marathon to Athens to announce that the Greeks had defeated the invading Persians in battle. The route was exhausting, and shortly after arriving in Athens Pheidippides fell to the ground dead.

In 1896, the first modern Olympic Games in Athens held a race of roughly the same length in his honour. It became known as the marathon.

MARATHON FACT FILE

- More than **400,000 people** in the USA compete in marathons annually.
- More than **800 marathons** are run in the world each year. The biggest marathons can have tens of thousands of runners.
- A marathon runner will go through **two pairs of trainers** while training for the race.
- Top marathon athletes will run **160 km** a week in training.
- It takes the average woman **51,214 steps** to complete a marathon.
- In 2008, 64-year-old Texan Larry Macon ran **105 marathons.**

Sand marathon

A competitor climbs a sand dune during the 2009 Marathon des Sables in the Sahara Desert. This desert marathon is considered the hardest in the world.

COOL RUNNING

Runners tackle rough mountain trails in the 2006 Everest Marathon. The starting line is at 5,180 m near Mount Everest Base Camp in Nepal, making it the highest marathon in the world.

HAVING A BALL

There are many ways to complete a marathon. This man at the 2008 Berlin Marathon was running in a sphere!

Bringing up the rear >>

Englishman Lloyd Scott walked the 2002 New York and London marathons wearing a 55-kg antique diving suit. In London, it took him five days and eight hours. In 2003, he wore the same suit to complete a marathon underwater!

STAYING POWER

Dave Heeley from England ran seven marathons on seven continents in seven days in 2008, even though he is blind.

Michal Kapral, from Toronto, Canada, ran a marathon in 3 hours 7 minutes in 2005 while juggling three balls at the same time.

Between 1997 and 2003, England's Robert Garside ran 48,000 km around the world in 2,062 days.

US soldier Jake Truex ran 5,000 m in just over 22 minutes in Germany in 2006 with a heavy 18-kg backpack strapped to his back.

Charlie Engle (USA), Ray Zahab (Canada) and Kevin Lin (Taiwan) ran the same distance as two marathons a day for 111 days to cross the 6,400-km Sahara Desert on foot in 2007. They had to cope with temperatures that were over 37°C by day, but below freezing at night.

FAST it it!

DID YOU KNOW?

At the London Marathon...

They use 710,000 bottles of water, 950 portable toilets, 500 stretchers and 68 ambulances.

The blue paint that marks out the course is steam-cleaned off as the last runner passes, so the streets of London can be quickly returned to normal.

Australia's Kurt Fearnley completed the 2009 race in a wheelchair in a record 1 hour 28 minutes 56 seconds.

The London Marathon was the first to be run over 26.2 miles. This is because at the 1908 Olympics the Royal Box lay 385 yards (350 m) beyond the 26-mile finish line. The race was extended so it could finish beneath the Royal Box.

RISKY BUSINESS

DANGEROUS SPORTS

Over the past 30 years, dozens of dangerous sports have been introduced that are exciting to do but, when things go wrong, can result in serious injury, even death. Only really physically fit people should attempt these sports – and even then they must have the right equipment, or the consequences could be fatal.

Cave divers plunge to depths of up to 30 m underwater in total darkness at the risk of losing their way or running out of air. Kayakers ride over the world's highest waterfalls, hitting terrifying speeds of 110 km/h on the way down. Bungee jumpers leap from bridges high above raging rivers with one end of an elastic cord tied to their ankles and the other end tied to the jumping-off point. For some people sport is only fun if they are putting their life at risk.

In the balance

This is not a trick photo. Eskil Ronningsbakken really is performing a one-handed handstand while balancing on the edge of a ladder attached to a 300-m-high cliff in Norway. He was able to do this by adding 150 kg of weights at the balancing end. It still looks pretty scary though.

SAY WHAT?

BASE JUMPING

BASE jumping is named after the places you jump from: **B**uildings (skyscrapers, statues), **A**ntennas (radio masts, cranes), **S**pans (bridges), and **E**arth (cliffs).

DEATH DEFYING

Have you ever wondered what it is like to be a hamster in a wheel? Well, the sport of Zorbing lets you find out. Zorbonauts roll down hills inside large transparent plastic spheres, reaching speeds of over 50 km/h.

CRAZY KAYAKING

One of the world's top extreme kayakers is fearless Jesse Combs from Oregon. Jesse risks life and limb by taking his kayak over steep crashing waterfalls such as this 20-m drop at the Mesa Falls in Idaho.

A NEED FOR SPEED

David Kirke, founder of England's Dangerous Sports Club, adapted a medieval rock-throwing device called a trebuchet so that humans could be catapulted 17 m into the air in under two seconds.

Bull running takes place in several Spanish towns, most famously in Pamplona. Participants have to run in front of a herd of angry bulls that have been let loose in the streets. Fifteen people have been killed in the Pamplona event since 1910.

Tyler Bradt paddled a kayak down the raging waters of the 33-m Alexandra Falls in Canada, and didn't flip once.

In 1991, John Kockelman made a bungee jump of 300 m from a hot-air balloon 1,500 m above California.

In BASE jumping, people hurl themselves from tall structures with just a parachute to save them from certain death. The thrill is to wait as long as possible before pulling the parachute cord. Here, leaping 280 m from the Menara Kuala Lumpur Tower in Malaysia, this jumper will have six seconds of freefall before he has to use his parachute.

People have **BASE jumped** from San Francisco's Golden Gate Bridge, the Eiffel Tower in Paris and New York City's Empire State Building.

In 2006, Australians Glenn Singleman and Heather Swan jumped off a **6,500-m-high** precipice on Meru Peak, India, and landed on a 5,000-m-high glacier.

In 2006, Dan Schilling made **201 BASE jumps** in 24 hours off a bridge 14 m above the Snake River Canyon, Idaho. He kept jumping even after fracturing his wrist.

An average of **15 people** are killed while BASE jumping every year.

TWIST it!

HAVING A BALL

Believe it or not, golf was the first sport to be played on the Moon. Astronaut Alan Shepard hit a couple of shots on the 1971 *Apollo 14* Moon mission. Ball games such as golf, bowling, pool and table tennis are played all over the world. Baseball also has a wide following, and an amazing 42 million people play it in the USA alone. Cricket is played in the UK, Australia, South Africa and Asia.

Most of these sports are over 100 years old, and some have their origins in ancient history. A form of bowling was played in Egypt as far back as 3200BC. The game was outlawed in England in 1366 because King Edward III wanted his soldiers to concentrate on archery practice instead.

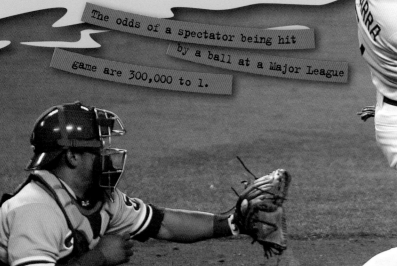

The odds of a spectator being hit by a ball at a Major League game are 300,000 to 1.

Nearly 80 million people pay to watch Major League baseball in a season.

Big teams like the New York Yankees average attendances of over 50,000 per game.

The athletic **Nomar Garciaparra** first starred for the Boston Red Sox in the 1990s. He is one of only a handful of players in Major League baseball history to have hit two grand slams (a home run hit when there are runners at three bases) during a single game.

UPSCALE BALL

Instead of being covered in leather, this cricket ball is covered in 2,704 diamonds. Made in Sri Lanka, it is said to be the first life-sized diamond-and-gold cricket ball in the world.

twist it!

Every Thanksgiving, Cincinnati, Ohio, hosts a Turkey Bowl, where competitors bowl frozen turkeys instead of bowling balls!

Playing baseball for Portsmouth High School, Ohio, in 2008, triplets Howard, John and Matt Harcha all hit home runs, in the order of their birth from oldest to youngest.

In 2007, English golfer David Huggins hit his third hole-in-one...and he was only eight years old.

Table tennis was first played in Victorian England in the 1880s on a dining room table, often using a cigar box lid as a bat, a champagne cork as a ball, and a row of books as a net!

PLAY BALL

English golfer Andrew Winfield teed off from the summit of Africa's Mount Kilimanjaro in 2008, 5,895 m above sea level.

CRICKET ODDITIES

● Cricket is played by two teams of 11 players. One team bowls and fields while the other bats. A team is in (at bat) until ten of its batsmen are out. Then the other team is in!

● Batsmen try to score runs by hitting the ball a long way. If a batsman is out for no runs, he has scored a duck — because zero is shaped like a duck's egg.

● The bowlers aim at three wooden stumps in the ground known as the wicket. They take it in turn to bowl 'overs', which consist of bowling six balls at the batsman. If no runs are scored off an over, it is called a maiden.

● There are ten ways a batsman can be out, including bowled, caught and leg before wicket (lbw).

BILLION-DOLLAR MAN

American golfer Tiger Woods became the first ever athlete to earn a billion dollars. He has won more than 70 tour events and when he was only three years old he shot an amazing score of 48 over nine holes at a golf club in California. He usually wears a red shirt on the final round of tournaments because he believes it helps him to win.

Perfect pitch

Jim Abbott was a Major League baseball pitcher in the 1990s even though he was born with only one hand. In 1993, playing for the New York Yankees, he even pitched a no-hitter (where the opposing team has no hits in an entire game) against the Cleveland Indians. This was a fantastic achievement because on average just two no-hitters a year have been thrown in Major League baseball since 1875.

WACKY RACES

FUN RUNS

You don't need an engine to take part in a wacky race, just a daft sense of humour. In various places across the world people push, pull or carry beds, toilets, coffins, even their wives – all in the name of sport.

For serious athletes who like a fun run, there is the mad dash up the stairs of the Empire State Building in New York. Germany's Thomas Dold won in 2006, 2007, 2008 and 2009, and he also excels at another crazy form of racing – running backwards!

BIRDS IN FLIGHT

Lightweight jockeys ride ostriches in a race in Shanghai, China. Ostrich racing is also popular in South Africa and in several locations in the USA. Ostriches can run at 72 km/h, the fastest running speed of any bird. Ostriches are harder to steer than horses, so although the jockeys have special saddles and reins, they still regularly fall off.

STEP UP THE PACE

Each year more than 300 runners take part in the race up the stairs of the Empire State Building. The climb to the observation deck is up 320 m, 86 floors, and 1,576 stairs. It takes most of the runners about 15 minutes to reach the observation deck. The building's elevator can get there in less than a minute.

DEAD FUNNY

Every year in Manitou Springs, Colorado, teams race coffins with a living female occupant. Around 40 coffins take part. They are rerunning the legend of Emma Crawford, who died in 1890 and was buried on top of Red Mountain, only to have her coffin slide down the canyon in 1929 after heavy rains.

Quackers!

More than 200,000 blue plastic ducks floated nearly a kilometre downstream on the River Thames in the 2009 Great British Duck Race. Each duck had a number, and people picked a duck, hoping that theirs would be the first to reach the finish and win them a cash prize.

IN IT TO WIN IT

People race decorated outdoor toilets through the streets of Dawson City in Canada! For the Great Klondike Outhouse Race, teams speed around a 2.4 km course. One person has to sit on the toilet the whole time!

In Sydney, Australia, there is a race solely for women wearing high stiletto-heeled shoes. The trick is to get to the finish line without spraining your ankle.

There's a Grand Prix in France that's just for homemade pedal cars. Drivers pump their legs around Valentigney for up to three hours, but design is just as important as speed. That's why you might see a man in a monkey mask driving a banana-shaped car!

How about doing the 100 m...on stilts? In the Philippines, competitors perch on top of 1.8-m stilts made of bamboo and walk along the course as fast as they can.

Marry and carry

Estonia's Madis Uusorg carries his wife Inga Klausen to victory in the 2007 Wife-carrying World Championships in Finland. The race is run over an obstacle course and the winner receives his wife's weight in beer.

¡in it 4si mi

FUN AND GAMES

OLYMPIC DREAMS

The Olympic Games are the greatest sporting show on earth. The ancient Olympics were held in Greece starting in the 8th century BC – nearly 3,000 years ago. Sports included the javelin, long jump, running in armour, and even kissing! After a long break, the Olympics were brought back in 1896 and are now held every four years. An incredible 4.5 billion people watched the 2008 Olympics in Beijing, China, either on TV or online.

In Beijing, more than 11,000 athletes from around 200 countries competed in more than 300 events, from athletics to wrestling. The Winter Olympics are just as exciting, featuring sports such as skiing, ice skating and bobsleigh. The winner of each event receives a gold medal, second place gets a silver medal, and third place gets a bronze medal. These are the most important prizes in sport.

STEVE REDGRAVE

A powerful rower, Britain's Steve Redgrave (second from left) in 2000 was one of only four Olympians to have won a gold medal at five consecutive Olympic Games.

Fan-tastic

To celebrate the 2008 Olympics in Beijing, a Chinese man, Dr. Wei Sheng, pierced his head, face, hands and chest with 2,008 needles in the five colours of the Olympic rings.

4,200 athletes from 148 countries took part in the 2008 Paralympics. These Games are for athletes with a physical disability or vision impairment. Sports include wheelchair basketball and wheelchair tennis.

EDWIN MOSES

Edwin Moses of the USA won gold in the 400 metres hurdles at both the 1976 and 1984 Olympics. Between 1977 and 1987 he was undefeated, winning a record 122 consecutive races.

US swimmer Michael Phelps won eight gold medals at the 2008 Beijing Olympics. It was the first time that this had been achieved by a competitor at a single Olympic Games.

Live pigeon shooting was an event at the 1900 Olympics. Nearly 300 birds were killed. It was the first and only time in Olympic history that animals were killed on purpose.

twist it!

GOING FOR GOLD

At the 1904 Olympics, George Eyser (USA) won six gymnastics medals, including three gold, despite having a wooden left leg.

Women were not allowed to compete in the Olympics track and field events at the Olympics until 1928. However, so many collapsed in that year that the 800 metres in the event was banned until at the end of 1960.

A 1956 Olympic water-polo match between Hungary and the USSR (modern-day Russia) was abandoned after the teams started fighting underwater.

After winning a rowing gold medal at the 1956 Olympics, 18-year-old Russian Vyacheslav Ivanov quickly lost it. He threw the medal into the air in celebration, but it landed in the lake. He dived in but was unable to find it.

The USA are the reigning Olympic rugby champions. That's because rugby was last featured in the Olympics in 1924 when the USA beat France 17–3 in the final.

Party time

The opening ceremony at the 2008 Beijing Olympics featured over 15,000 performers and a spectacular display of 35,000 fireworks. The four-hour ceremony cost £70 million – that's nearly £5,000 per second – making it the most expensive in Olympic history.

CLARA HUGHES

Canada's Clara Hughes is one of only a few athletes to win medals at both the Summer and Winter Olympics. She succeeded at both cycling and speed skating.

MICHAEL PHELPS

INDEX

ACKNOWLEDGEMENTS

COVER (t/l) © Speedfighter – Fotolia.com, (c) © Diego Cervo – Fotolia.com, (c/l) © Feng Yu – Fotolia.com, (t) © Albo – Fotolia.com, (b/r) www.jw-sportfoto.de; **2** (b) Reuters/Claro Cortes, (t) Anja Niedringhaus/AP/Press Association Images; **3** Georges Christen; **4** (b/l) © Michael Lawlor – Fotolia.com, (b/c) © kamphi – Fotolia.com, (t) iStock.com, (b/r) © Terry Morris – Fotolia.com; **5** (t/r) © Thomas Lammeyer – iStock.com, (b/l) © Michael Lawlor – Fotolia.com, (b/cl, b/c, b/cr) N & B – Fotolia.com, (b/r) Pawel Nowik – Fotolia.com, (r) © Feng Yu – Fotolia.com; **6** (b/l) Reuters/United Photos; **6–7** (dp) Reuters/Stringer USA; **7** (r) Anja Niedringhaus/AP/Press Association Images; **8** Reuters/Stefano Rellandini; **9** (t/l) Reuters/Fahad Shadeed, (b/r) Reuters/Claro Cortes, (b) Reuters/Chaiwat Subprasom; **10** (l) Phil Walter/Getty Images, (t/r, c) Michael Martin/Barcroft Media Ltd, (b/r) © Chepko Danil – iStock.com; **11** (r) John Chapple/Rex Features, (t/l) Tony Gentile/Reuters, (b/r) Reuters Photographer/Reuters; **12** William Tremblay wl_tremblay@hotmail.com; **13** (t/l) Archive Photos/Getty Images, (b/r) Georges Christen; **14** (b/r) Mike Hewitt/Getty Images; **14–15** (t) Nathaniel S. Butler/NBAE/Getty Images; **15** (b/l) © Thomas Lammeyer – iStock.com, (b/r) Toby Melville/Reuters, (c) David E. Klutho/Sports Illustrated/Getty Images; **16** (t) © Pierre Jacques/Hemis/Corbis, (b) Gary Caskey/Reuters; **17** (t/r) Reuters/Yuriko Nakao, (t/l) © Reuters/Corbis, (r) S Levy/Getty Images; **18** (l) Sam Yeh/AFP/Getty Images, (t/l) Reuters Photographer/Reuters; **18–19** Sam Yeh/AFP/Getty Images; **19** (t/l) Heribert Proepper/AP/Press Association Images, (b/r) © Julien Rousset – Fotolia.com; **20** (l) David Purdy/Landov/Press Association Images, (r) © George Peters – iStock.com; **20–21** (dp) © Peter Baxter – Fotolia.com; **21** (t/l) Lynne Cameron/PA Wire/Press Association Images, (l) Jonathan Daniel/Getty Images, (b/r) Damien Meyer/AFP/Getty Images; **22** Lester Lefkowitz/Corbis; **23** (l) seanwhite.net/Sean White Photography, (r) AFP/Getty Images; **24** (t/l, t/r, c, b, r) Rex Features; **25** (t/l) Barcroft Media via Getty Images, (t/r) Barcroft Media Ltd; **26** (t) © Maxym Boner – iStock.com, (l) © Arturo Limon – iStock.com, (b/r) © Bart Sadowski – iStock.com; **27** (l) Alfaqui/Barcroft Media Ltd, (t/r) Samantha Sin/AFP/Getty Images, (r) Ermann J. Knippertz/AP/Press Association Images; **28–29** (c) Doug Pensinger/Getty Images, (b) Anthony Acosta; **29** (b/l) www.jw-sportfoto.de, (b/r) ChinaFotoPress/Cheng Jiang/Photocome/Press Association Images, (t/r) © Simon de Trey-White/Barcroft Pacific; **30** (t/l) Reuters/Christian Hartmann, (c) Johnny Green/PA Wire/Press Association Images; **30–31** (dp) Stephen Pond/Empics Sport; **31** (t/l) Wenn, (t) Kin Cheung/AP/Press Association Images, (t/r) © Reuters/Corbis, (b/r) © EuroPics [CEN], (b/l) Rex Features; **32** © Daniel Ramsbott/epa/Corbis; **33** (b/l, b) © Axel Koester/Corbis, (t/l) Sam Barcroft/Rex Features, (r) © Daniel Cardiff – iStock.com; **34** Neale Haynes/Rex Features; **35** (l) Warren Bolster, (r) © Don Bayley – iStock.com, (b/l) Denis Poroy/AP/Press Association Images, (b/r) John Hugg: mauisurfboard.com; huggsmaui.com; **36** Pierre Verdy/Getty Images; **37** (l) Getty Images, (t) Reuters/Str New, (c) Reuters/Pawel Kopczynski; **38** (sp) Sindre Lundvold/Barcroft Media, (b/r) Sipa Press/Rex Features; **39** (l) Photograph by Darin Quoid, (t/r) © Jörg Hackemann – Fotolia.com; **40** (sp) Paul Spinelli/MLB Photos via Getty Images, (b/r) Sena Vidanagama/Stringer/Getty Images; **41** (t/r) iStock.com, (b/l) John Zich/AFP/Getty Images, (b/r) Dave Martin/AP/Press Association Images; **42** (b/l) Reuters/Brendan Mcdermid, (b/r) Andra DuRee Martin; **42–43** (t) Reuters/Nir Elias; **43** (l) Reuters/Lehtikuva Lehtikuva, (t/r) Jonathan Hordle/Rex Features, (t) © Michael Flippo – iStock.com; **44** ((b/l) Sipa Press/Rex Features, (c) ChinaFotoPress/Photocome/Press Association Images; **44–45** (dp) © Luc Santerre Castonguay – iStock.com, (t/r) Bob Jones/Rex Features; **45** (b) Reuters/Staff Photographer, (l) Rex Features, (b/r) Reuters/Max Rossi

Key: t = top, b = bottom, c = centre, l = left, r = right, sp = single page, dp = double page, bgd = background

All other photos are from Ripley's Entertainment Inc. All artwork by Rocket Design (East Anglia) Ltd.

Every attempt has been made to acknowledge correctly and contact copyright holders and we apologise in advance for any unintentional errors or omissions, which will be corrected in future editions.

TWISTS